# Saving

| Contents | Page |
|---|---|
| Giant pandas | 2-3 |
| Danger | 4-5 |
| Bamboo | 6-7 |
| Forests | 8-9 |
| Reservations | 10-11 |
| Zoos | 12-13 |
| Baby pandas | 14-15 |
| Saving giant pandas | 16 |

written by John Lockyer

giant panda

Giant pandas are very big bears. Their faces are white with black patches around their eyes.

They have short tails and thick coats of black and white fur.

Giant pandas are in danger of disappearing from the world. The only place they are found is in the high mountains of China.

Giant pandas like cool, wet, forests that are full of bamboo plants. Bamboo is the food they like best.

They eat and eat for most of the day. Their front paws have five fingers and a special thumb to hold the bamboo.

bamboo

People in China think there are only about two thousand giant pandas living there. They are almost extinct.

Giant pandas are disappearing because the bamboo forests are being cut down. People want the wood from the trees and they want the land for farms.

forest

Then the giant pandas will have nothing at all left to eat.
If they can't find new forests with bamboo, they will starve.

*reservation*

Now many people in China are trying to save the giant pandas. There are special places in the mountains called reservations. The bears are very safe there, because nobody can cut down trees or hurt them.

Zoos in some other countries are trying to save giant pandas, too. There are only about two hundred giant pandas in zoos.

Reservations and zoos are the only places in the world where people can see giant pandas.

When baby pandas are born in zoos, they are looked after very carefully.

*panda cub*

The zookeepers and the mother pandas help the cubs to grow strong.

Zoos and reservations are working hard to save the giant pandas.